Map of

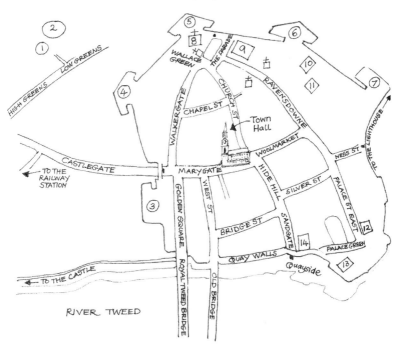

Key
1. Bell Tower (1557)
2. Lord's Mount (1540)
3. Meg's Mount
4. Cumberland Bastion
5. Brass Bastion
6. Windmill Bastion
7. King's Mount
8. Parish Church (1642)
9. Barracks (1721)
10. Gunpowder Magazine (1749)
11. Lions House
12. Governor's House
13. Main Guard (1815)
14. Customs House

A word about Anne and Cara

ANNE BRUCE ENGLISH first saw Berwick as a child, through a train window, travelling from Newcastle to Edinburgh. Years later she visited the town, looking into family links with Holy Island and Berwick upon Tweed. From these visits, and from walks around the town in all weathers, her fondness for Berwick grew and led to this book.

The first book in this series, also written by Anne, is *Let's Explore Edinburgh Old Town*. These books will appeal to children and families, with their mix of facts, stories and quizzes.

Anne has written widely for children, including stories, poems and dramatised scripts for BBC Education (Radio), both London and Edinburgh based. Her work is included in many anthologies and she has also written feature articles for magazines and newspapers

She and her husband now live in Edinburgh. They have two daughters and an elderly cat called Mitzi Dundee.

CARA LOCKHART SMITH is an illustrator and writer of children's books and lives in Berwick upon Tweed. Much of her recent work has been inspired by the town, including a widely distributed pictorial map.

Her studio is inhabited by a stuffed barn owl, a rocking metal whale and a lot of organised chaos.

She is currently working on a book featuring the Berwick bear.

To Lucy and Jim
Enjoy reading this

Let's Explore

BERWICK

upon Tweed

Anne Bruce English.

Cara Lockhart Smith

Anne Bruce English

Maps and illustrations by
Cara Lockhart Smith

Luath Press Limited
EDINBURGH

www.luath.co.uk

First published 2003

The paper used in this book is acid-free,
neutral-sized and recyclable. It is made from low
chlorine pulps produced in a low energy, low
emission manner from sustainable forests.

Printed and bound by J. W. Arrowsmith Ltd, Bristol

Designed by Tom Bee, Edinburgh

Typeset by Helen Johnston Publishing Services,
Berwick upon Tweed (01289 307626)

Contents

Acknowledgements

My thanks to all who helped with my enquiries, including Linda Bankier, Borough Archivist; staff at the Public Library; the Civic Society (especially for the annual feast of Doors Open days); Revd Alan Hughes, Holy Trinity Church; staff of the Tourist Information Centre; James Allan, Curator, Town Hall; Chris Green, Curator of the Borough Museum; and English Heritage for the By Beat of Drum exhibition. Berwick booksellers also gave welcome advice.

Thanks are also due to Lorna Suthren, Tourism Resources Officer, Derek Smibert, Chairman of the North Northumberland Tourism Association and Chris Green for reading the typescript of this book.

The Town of Berwick

Quick Quiz Is Berwick nearer to Newcastle or Edinburgh? *Answer on page 12.*

The Town of Berwick – English or Scottish?

Travelling north from London to Edinburgh, Berwick is now the last town in England. But it has also been the first town in Scotland. For hundreds of years it was right on the wild frontier between two countries who were often at war.

The town changed hands 14 times in 300 years. Since 1482 it has been an English town. But the border with Scotland is only 5km (3 miles) away.

There are still grumbles from some people in Scotland that Berwick should be a Scottish town again, so the arguing might not be over. It's not long since a Scotsman stood on the Old Bridge at Berwick holding a sign that read SCOTLAND. For him, that's where Scotland begins.

Fighting Facts

The worst time for the people of Berwick was between 1296 and 1333. In these years terrible events happened, among them a massacre, an execution and a huge battle.

1. **The Massacre** – Berwick was a Scottish town in 1296 when King Edward I of England, nicknamed Longshanks because of his height, invaded the country. He was the victor. He ordered that all the men of the town should be put to death. It's said that 7,000 were killed on Good Friday, 30 March 1296, and that the town ran with blood.

   Edward started rebuilding Berwick castle and building new town walls to keep out the Scots. It's said he wheeled the first barrowload of earth himself. Edward was king for 35 years and until the day he died he fought the Scots. No wonder the words 'Here lies Edward the Hammer of the Scots' were carved on his tomb.

2. **An Execution** – The Scottish leader William Wallace raised an army to fight King Edward. He was successful to begin with but then Edward defeated him. Wallace escaped and hid but someone betrayed him.

   At his trial in London he was found guilty of treason and executed. The horrible habit in those days was for the body to be cut up and pieces displayed in public. William Wallace's head was stuck on a spike on London Bridge. It's believed that part of his body was brought to Berwick to be displayed as a warning to others.

3. **The Battle of Halidon Hill** – It was Edward III who marched his troops to Halidon Hill in

1333. The hill is just north of Berwick, off the road to Duns. From the top of the hill the English troops had a good view of the Scottish soldiers as they struggled through boggy ground. The English army cut them down with a hail of arrows as they climbed uphill. The Scots surrendered.

4. **Bodies and Bones** – After a battle, ordinary prisoners were sometimes killed and buried. (Wealthy noblemen would be held to ransom and returned home if the ransom money was paid.) Bodies and bones have been dug up all over Berwick. Some were soldiers. Others are from old graveyards. When the reservoir in Castlegate was being dug, cartloads of bones were found and thrown away. Other bones, including skulls, were found inside houses. Even in 1998, skeletons were dug up in Castle Terrace when a new house was going to be built. Building work was stopped.

Berwick now –
English and Scottish

There's an old rhyme about Berwick:

> They talk about England and Scotland
> indeed
> But it's England and Scotland and Berwick
> upon Tweed.

Berwick is different. Although it's in England now it is a mixture of both countries.

- Berwick has branches of English banks and Scottish banks.
- You can spend English banknotes and Scottish ones.
- You can buy English newspapers and Scottish newspapers.
- There are English churches and Scottish churches.
- The mayor of Berwick wears purple robes, the colour used in Scotland, and not the scarlet robes of England.
- Strangest of all is the football club, Berwick Rangers. Their home ground is in England but the team play as part of the Scottish League.

Quick Quiz answer Berwick is nearer to Edinburgh (91km/57 miles) than it is to Newcastle (104km/64 miles).

The Berwick Name and Bear

Quick Quiz You'll meet a rebus here. Is this a kind of puzzle or a kind of bear? *Answer on page 14 .*

The Name

Berwick upon Tweed probably means 'the barley farm on the River Tweed'. 'Bere' was the old name for barley.

There's good farming land all around Berwick and grain was brought into the town and stored in huge granaries. It was then sold and it brought wealth to the town.

The Bear

The Borough coat of arms tells us a different story about the name. It shows a bear chained to a tree. The bear gives us the 'Ber' in Berwick. The tree is a wych elm. It gives the 'wick' in Berwick. So we have Ber-wick. Someone is having fun with words.

Three places to find the coat of arms

1. *On the front of the town hall. It's a new plastic copy made for the Millennium Year, 2000.*

2. *Close by, on the police station in Church Street. It's set in an arch high on the wall.*

3. *On the Borough offices on Wallace Green. It has two chained bears, one sitting and one standing.*

Berwick stories in this book have a picture of a bear beside them.

Quick Quiz answer A rebus is a puzzle, using pictures instead of words. The coat of arms is a rebus.

15

The River Tweed and Berwick's Swans

Quick Quiz A male swan is called a cob. A female swan is a pen. A young swan is a cygnet. Is a group of swans called a herd or a gaggle? *Answer on page 17.*

The River Tweed

The River Tweed is 155km long. It starts at Tweed's Well, in the Scottish Borders, and reaches the sea at Berwick upon Tweed. The river has been a problem and a blessing for the town. In the fighting years it was a problem because Berwick could be attacked from the sea. It's also a shallow river and floods easily. Bridges across the river have been damaged or even washed away by floods or ice.

It has been a blessing because Tweed salmon brought wealth to the town. The salmon was packed in Berwick and sold. Some of it went by ship to London.

The harbour brought ships and trade to the town. Berwick harbour is quiet now, but the harbour at **Tweedmouth** across the river still has a salmon fishery and there is boatbuilding at Tweed Dock.

The river is also home to Berwick's famous swans.

The Swans

Berwick swans are the kind called mute swans.
They do make grunting noises and hiss when
they're angry. The birds can be fierce when they
have young ones. It's best not to get too close
as they strike with their powerful wings.

- **Why Berwick?** There have been swans in
  Berwick for 60 or 70 years. Swans are
  vegetarian and they stay in Berwick because
  there is plenty for them to eat. They eat
  seaweed in the shallow water close to the
  pier, and river plants near the three bridges.
  People feed them too, although that's not
  always a good thing. If you do feed them
  bread, then brown bread is better for them
  than soggy white.

- **How many swans?** In July and August there
  can be up to 800 swans at Berwick. Many of
  them leave later in the year.

- **Safety.** Once a year swans moult – they lose
  all their flight feathers at once. For four to six
  weeks they can't fly so they need somewhere
  safe to rest and sleep. As well as food they
  find safety in Berwick. You'll see them resting
  in the harbour and close to the bridges.

- **Danger.** Water pollution is the worst danger
  they face. Over 200 were killed in Berwick in
  1986 when vandals let oil into the water. They
  can also choke on lead weights and fishing
  lines left in the water. The Berwick Swan and
  Wildlife Trust was started after the 1986 oil
  pollution. The Trust treats swans who have
  been hurt in any way.

- **Counting swans.** Eighty swans survived the
  oil pollution. They were the first to be 'ringed'

at Berwick. Swans ringed at Berwick have a white leg ring and a ring with a number. They act like a swan ID card. It's easier to count the swans and to check how far they travel when they have been ringed.

More Swan Facts

Berwick swans are wild and free. No one owns them.

Swans are heavy birds and weigh between 8 and 12kg.

They live for about seven years.

There are no nesting swans in Berwick – they nest in other places.

A long time ago swans were kept for food and eaten on feast days.

Quick Quiz answer A group of swans is a herd. It's a gaggle of geese.

Berwick's Bridges

Quick Quiz Berwick lies on the A1 road. What does A1 stand for? What is another name for the road? *Answers on page 21.*

Three Famous Bridges in 300 Years

- The oldest is nearly 400 years old. Road traffic still uses it.

- The next is 150 years old. It takes all the rail traffic on the main east coast line.

- The newest is about 75 years old. It carries some road traffic away from Berwick's narrow streets.

Berwick Bridge – The Old Bridge

1. It was begun in 1611 and finished in 1634, so it took 24 years, 4 months and 4 days to build.

2. 300 men (and a few women) worked on it.

3. It has 15 arches.

4. It's built of local pink sandstone.

Bridge Tales

Earlier bridges at Berwick either fell down or were washed away by floods and ice. When James I visited Berwick he was afraid to cross the shaky old bridge. At last he gave money to build a new one.

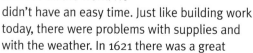

James Burrell was the master mason for this bridge. He was paid 2s 6d (35p) a day to oversee all the work. He didn't have an easy time. Just like building work today, there were problems with supplies and with the weather. In 1621 there was a great flood that washed away months of work.

The bridge is still as he built it – a narrow road bridge with passing places for people on foot.

Can you guess? There's an old saying, 'The middle of Berwick Bridge is at one end.' What can it mean?

Answer The highest arch of the bridge is not in the middle. It's the second arch from the Berwick end. This is where the water is deepest. The high arch lets boats sail through the deep water channel.

The Royal Border Bridge – the Railway Bridge

1. Begun in 1847, finished in 1850.

2. 2,000 men worked on it.

3. It has 28 arches, only 12 are over water and the other 16 are on dry land.

4. It's built of limestone, bricks and hard American elm wood.

Bridge Tales

The bridge is a viaduct, carrying the railway across the valley. The bridge curves and is tall and elegant. The designer was the famous Robert Stephenson. It got the *Royal* name because Queen Victoria declared it open on 29 August 1850.

Can you guess? How long did Queen Victoria stay in Berwick that day – 12 minutes, 24 minutes or 60 minutes?

Answer She stayed for only 12 minutes and she didn't make a speech.

The Royal Tweed Bridge – The New Bridge

1. Begun in 1925, finished in 1928.

2. Nearly 3,000 men and 180 horses worked on it.

3. It has 4 arches.

4. It's built mainly of concrete.

Bridge Tales

This is a wide road bridge. It was improved in 1999–2000 when it was given wider pavements and new lighting. Parking on the bridge was stopped.

There's a bronze plaque at each end – the arms of England at the south end and the arms of Scotland at the north end.

It's another *Royal* bridge because it was opened, on a cold and wet day in May, by the then Prince of Wales, Queen Victoria's great grandson. He did make a speech.

Can you guess? How old was the oldest person invited to the opening – 85 years, 90 years or 95 years old?

Answer 95 years old. Twenty-one people who

saw Queen Victoria open the Royal Border Bridge were invited back. That was 78 years later. They had a photograph taken looking very cold and wearing heavy coats and big hats. Most of them carried umbrellas and walking sticks.

Berwick got another bridge in 1983 as part of the A1 bypass road. Road and bridge take more heavy traffic away from the town.

Quick Quiz answer A1 means the road was the most important one in the whole country. (This was before the motorway 'M' roads.) The A1 joined the capital cities of London and Edinburgh and it made Berwick a busy place. The other name for the A1 was the Great North Road.

The Elizabethan Walls

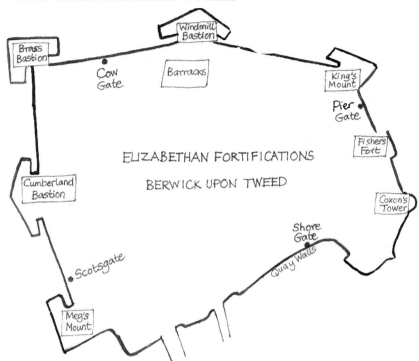

Meg's Mount. Called after a huge cannon which stood here.

Cumberland Bastion. Named after the Duke of Cumberland, victor over the Scots at the Battle of Culloden, who marched through Berwick in 1746.

Brass Bastion. It did have a brass cannon on it.

Windmill Bastion. A high and windy place. A windmill stood here in the 16th century.

King's Mount. The King may have been James I, travelling south for his coronation in 1603.

Quick Quiz Was 'Roaring Meg' a big gun or a woman with a loud voice? *Answer on page 25.*

The Elizabethan Walls prove that Berwick was an important town right on the wild frontier. Queen Elizabeth I spent more money on them than any other defence project in her long reign. She was queen for 44 years, and spent 22 years building Berwick's Walls.

Elizabeth was afraid of the Scots, but also of the French and the Spanish. Berwick had to be protected from them all. The Elizabethan Walls were built higher and stronger than Berwick's Edwardian Walls, and this time there were guns on them. Built in the 16th century, they are still standing in the 21st century.

Walking the Walls

Look for:

- **Lady Jerningham's statue** on Meg's Mount. She's the lady with the dogs and is looking towards her home, Longridge Towers.

- The remains of the cobbled sentry walk at **Brass Bastion**.

- **Windmill Bastion**, the highest place on the Walls, so it was a good place for a windmill.

- **Kipper Hill**. The path from King's Mount to Pier Gate is next to Kipper Hill. The long building with the red roof was a smokehouse where herring were smoked.

Building the Walls

1. **The Wall or Ramparts.** Workmen dug a ditch and piled up the earth behind it for the Walls. They could be 7 metres/50 feet thick and the front was faced with stone. The Walls were so strong that you can still walk along them after 400 years.

2. **The Ditch.** This was a sneaky bit of building. The ditch in front of part of the Walls was filled with shallow water. But halfway across there was a deeper ditch, 2.5 metres/18 feet deep. Anyone trying to wade across it could drown.

3. **The Gun Postions or Bastions.** Five strong gun positions were built on the Walls. The guns could fire forwards and along the Walls. In the 16th century this was as up-to-date as 20th-century rockets and guided missiles.

All the gun positions have names. The three biggest are **Cumberland, Brass** and **Windmill** Bastions. They're shaped like wide arrowheads. The two smaller ones, **Meg's Mount** and **King's Mount,** are like half arrowheads. Together they guarded the town from attack by land, sea or river.

Four fortified gates were built through the Walls – **Scotsgate, Cow Gate, Pier Gate** and **Shoregate** – so the people of Berwick could get in and out of the town.

Question The Walls were never finished, but were they any use?

Answer We'll never know because they were not needed.

When Queen Elizabeth died in 1603, her heir was King James VI of Scotland. Since then the two countries have shared a king or queen. There have been threats of invasion, but no one has invaded Berwick.

On Sentry Duty – A Dangerous Business

There used to be a cobbled sentry path round the Elizabethan Walls. You can still see it at Brass Bastion. Sentries patrolled day and night, looking and listening for possible attack. Darkness was the dangerous time, when an attack was most likely. The Captain of the Guard walked the Walls each night and any sentry found dozing was punished. This is what could happen to him:

The sentry was put in a basket with bread, water and a knife. The basket was hung over the Wall on a rope and left there. After a set time the sentry was allowed to cut the rope and he fell into the shallow ditch. Then he had to clamber out, wet, cold and ashamed. He would stay awake the next time he was on sentry duty.

Snakes Alive!

The seats along the Walls are supported on cast iron snakes. The snake's head, with its long tongue, is under the seat. The body and forked tail curl up behind the back rest.

Quick Quiz answer It was the name of a big gun, a 'Roaring Meg', which stood on Meg's Mount.

The Four Gates, Guns and More Guns

Quick Quiz Why did cows go through the Cow Gate? *Answer on page 28.*

The Four Gates

The Gates were very important to Berwick when it was a town on the wild frontier. They were built as tunnels through the Elizabethan Walls, with strong wooden doors inside which could be closed and locked. The doors kept enemies outside the Walls and the people of the town safe inside.

Even after England and Scotland shared the same king there were years of danger ahead for Berwick. Sometimes England was at war with France or Spain. Later, there was danger from the Scottish Jacobites who wanted Bonnie Prince Charlie to be king.

Four Gates
(they're marked on the map of the Walls on page 22)

1. **Scotsgate** guarded the main road leading to the north and to Scotland. It's the oldest entrance gate, in use from 1590. It's been rebuilt and widened to cope with the heavy traffic but tall vehicles still have to drive through in the middle of the road.

The Main Guard building was close to Scotsgate. It was used by soldiers on guard duty. When the Gate was locked overnight the soldiers decided

who was let through and who wasn't. A doctor on call was usually let through, although not always. Carriages, carts and anyone on horseback were not. It was better not to argue with the guard or they could keep you waiting for hours, or even turn you roughly away.

2. **Cow Gate**, off the Parade. Cows did go through this narrow Gate, taken out to grass in the morning and brought inside the Walls for safety at night. Cow Gate has not been altered since it was built in 1596, but the wooden doors are much newer. There was a second pair of doors, and a portcullis, a kind of sliding gate which could be dropped down very quickly. The town was well protected here.

3. **Pier Gate** is the newest (1816), built so that traffic could reach the pier and lighthouse which are outside the Elizabethan Walls.

4. **Shoregate**, on the quayside, was important because it protected the town from attack by sea. It still has two of the heavy wooden doors put there when Shoregate was built in the 1760s. They're shaped to fit the arched roof of the tunnel.

MISSING! *Bridge Gate or English Gate was at the Berwick end of the Old Bridge. It guarded the road from the south. When Berwick was a Scottish town this gate would keep out the English if they attacked by land. The Gate was taken down in 1825.*

Guns and More Guns

The nearer you get to the harbour the more places there on the Walls for guns. They were there to fire on attackers coming by sea.

How many guns? Answer below.

1. **Fisher's Fort,** opposite the long green of The Avenue, had six guns. The gun there now is a Russian cannon from the Crimean War.

2. **The Four Gun Battery,** close to Coxon's Tower. The tower is a high look-out post with a good view out to sea and down the coast. The tower is safe and easy to climb.

3. **The Saluting Battery,** in front of the three tall houses of Wellington Terrace, had places for 13 guns.

4. **The Eight Gun Battery** is nearest to Quay Walls. Despite the name, it now has places for nine guns. The stone gun platforms are covered with grass but you can see where they were and count them.

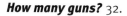

How many guns? 32.

Quick Quiz answer Cows were taken through the Cow Gate to grass in the morning and brought back at night.

Quay Walls and the Harbour

Danger – Beware of dive-bombing seagulls.

Quick Quiz These mystery objects are outside number 7 Quay Walls (a house) and number 4 (offices). What were they used for? *Answer on page 31.*

Quay Walls

After the gates and the guns, Quay Walls is peaceful and not at all warlike. The doors of the houses open onto the path along the Walls. All the houses are different – different heights, widths and colours. About 30 years ago some of them were almost in ruins. Doors and windows were broken and tiles falling off the roofs. The Berwick Town Preservation Trust, with other help, began rebuilding or repairing them. Their work goes on in the town today.

On Quay Walls look for:

- **21 Quay Walls,** with pale green walls and long venetian windows on the first and second floors. The artist Thomas Sword Good lived here. He painted pictures of fishermen and views of the coast. His portrait of local strongman Jimmy Strength shows a hunched, ragged and frightening old man. The story of Jimmy Strength is on page 45.

- **8 Quay Walls** is the Customs House. There's a royal coat of arms above the door and a flagpole on the wall. When Berwick was a busy port, customs officers were kept hard at work. They had to check all the goods arriving or leaving by sea. Duty had to be paid on everything, from iron, coal and wood to oranges, wine and candles.
- Look outside **number 7** and **number 4** Quay Walls for the mystery object.

Quay Walls ends at the Old Bridge but the walk can go on by **Bridge Terrace** to the path along by the river and under two bridges. The high road climbs **Bankhill** to Meg's Mount and the Elizabethan Walls.

The Harbour

Quay Walls looks down on the quayside and harbour. This was the working heart of old Berwick. Smacks, sloops, schooners and clipper ships used the harbour. They all had masts and sails. Cargoes were loaded and unloaded here and passengers waited to sail to London on the fast Berwick smacks. It was cheaper than travelling by stagecoach, and some travellers felt it was safer. Just in case of attack, the ships did carry guns and ammunition.

Cargoes sailing out of Berwick (exported) included salmon, grain, wool, stockings and eggs. Eggs were a strange cargo. They were collected from the countryside every day by egglers then packed in straw in wooden chests and shipped to London. Most of the eggs were used by bakers. In one year, up to 8 million eggs were exported.

Cargoes sailing into Berwick (imported)

included flax, tobacco, nails, bricks and ice. There's more about ice and Berwick's ice houses on pages 83–84 .

Today the quayside is quiet and empty, but there's one survivor of the busy times. Close to the black signpost is the Little Dock. This is where the earlier quayside ended. A few small boats may be tied up here. Eight or nine steep steps in the wall of the dock lead down to the water. Passengers may have used them to board their ship. It would never be easy using the narrow and slippery steps wearing old-style clothes.

Spooky Sallyport

Above a tunnel entrance on the quayside is the name 'Sallyport'. This is a creepy place. The tunnel is narrow with a low stone roof. Because it curves you can't see from one end to the other so it is dark. You feel very much alone walking through it.

It was built like this so that soldiers guarding the harbour could rush out and surprise anyone planning to attack from the quayside. It's another survivor of the wild frontier days.

Quick Quiz answer The mystery objects are boot-scrapers. They were used to scrape mud, dirt and horse dung off your shoes before you went into the house.

Trapped in the Ice –
The Last Voyage
of the Whaling Ship 'Norfolk'

The biggest ships to sail from Berwick were two whaling ships, the *Lively* and the *Norfolk*. Each year they sailed beyond the Arctic Circle to hunt for whales. The *Lively* was lost at sea in 1825. The *Norfolk* left Berwick in 1836 but became trapped in the ice. It was May 1837 before she reached home again.

This was before the days of radio and radar. For the men's families there was only silence – and rumours in Berwick that the *Norfolk* had sunk. This is the story of that trip which a crewman could have told his family when he was home again.

'Once we pass the tip of Greenland the trouble can start. We sail as far as the ice will let us, and then we set about our task. On this voyage we soon caught three whales so we were kept busy.

It's a bleak place to work. There's no land to be seen, north, south, east or west. We work in darkness, and it's so cold.

Then the icebergs began to gather round us, as high as cliffs. There was still open water between them, so we weren't trapped. But by the middle of January it all grew worse. We met pack ice, gigantic solid walls of ice pressing closer and closer. Then we were trapped.

That pack ice could have crushed us as easily as a boot crushing a beetle, and the Norfolk *was the beetle.*

I've never told you this before, but pack ice terrifies me. It cracks and groans and crashes. The huge blocks tumble over and over. The noise is deafening. I feel it's alive, that it's out to get me, to drown me in the icy water.

For two months out there I kept a diary, afraid I would never see you and Berwick again. This is what I wrote in my diary:

Today the sun shone for the first time in eight weeks. We sat on deck, and out came the concertina and the tin whistles. We sang and joked. Now we all feel better.

No sun today. Food is scarce so we must eat less. Already I hate our salt beef and dry bread. Some of the men are sick. They have ulcers on their legs and in their mouths.

The ice came even closer today. We put our sick men into a boat in case we had to abandon ship. They are too ill to walk.

Today Captain Thompson told us to pack our seachests and be ready to leave the ship. Thank God the ice came no closer so we are still on board.

A bad day. We've little coal left and even less to eat. Five of our men are very ill. The rest of us are so weary that we can barely move. What will become of us?

At last! After two months trapped in this wretched place, the ice has parted and we have sailed clear of it. Not many of us can work so everything is done slowly. We can stand watch for one hour but not for four.

We've reached the open sea! I dare dream of home again. Of the fifty men and boys who sailed with us, eight have now died.

'Today we're home again. Berwick has given us a great welcome back. As we neared the harbour we could see the crowds lining the Walls. We heard cheering, then the town hall bells began to ring. Then friends on shore pulled on the rope to draw us in.

*Now I'm back on dry land, I can hardly stand.
My time at sea is up. I'm not sailing again.'*

This was a wise decision. The *Norfolk* was sold
to a Hull firm after this voyage. She did make
one more journey, but not from Berwick. Once
again she was trapped in ice near the Arctic
Circle. This time she did not get free. The
Norfolk and all her crew were lost.

This story is based on records held in Berwick Record
Office. [BRO.695 and BRO.367/3]

Bridge Street, Stagecoaches and Carriers' Carts

Quick Quiz If you were given a Berwick cockle would you (a) eat it (b) take it out of a shell and then eat it? *Answer on page 37.*

Bridge Street

This narrow street is one of the oldest in Berwick and it was one of the busiest. It leads to the Old Bridge and all traffic had to use the street to cross the River Tweed.

It's also close to the harbour, so Bridge Street was one of the best places to live for wealthy merchants and wharfingers (wharf owners). They could keep an eye on business at the quayside.

Lanes, alleyways and yards link Bridge Street with the quayside. Coopers worked in some of the yards making barrels, called kitts, for the fish trade. In **Dewar's Lane** there was a five-storey granary, close to the harbour for loading the grain on board ship. The empty building is still there. The walls lean inwards and plants grow from the walls. The lane is narrow, just the width for a horse and cart.

Secrets and smugglers

The Old Bridge Tavern stood in Bridge Street, where the small car park is now. When the tavern was pulled down in 1963 a secret was uncovered. Hidden behind a fireplace was an old painted wall. Very few of these 16th-century walls have survived. The Berwick wall is black and white, covered with a strange mixture of pictures. Among them are flowers, cherubs and demons. It's now in the Borough Museum.

Workmen also found well-built tunnels under the building. The story is that smugglers used the tunnels to avoid paying custom duty. Tobacco, wine and spirits did arrive in Berwick by sea, and there were sometimes smugglers in Berwick gaol.

Bridge Street now

1. **Shoe Lane**. There was a shoe shop here with a shoe factory behind it. A piece of the old machinery is in the courtyard.

2. New in 2000 was the Backpackers' Hostel. It has had visitors from Britain, Australia, New Zealand, India, Sweden and Spain.

Sandgate with Hide Hill

If the quayside was the place to start your journey by sea, Sandgate and Hide Hill were important for another kind of journey – a journey by road.

Two of Berwick's three coaching inns were here. The smallest, the Hen and Chickens, is still in Sandgate. Hide Hill had a bigger coaching inn, the King's Arms, which is also still there. It had its own stables and even kept a spare coach for emergencies. While the tired horses were changed, passengers had half an hour for supper, then they set out again. An armed guard travelled with them. On the open roads there was always the danger of highwaymen.

A plaque on the wall of the King's Arms gives the dates when the writer Charles Dickens stayed there. Across the road, the building with the curved front (now Popinjays) was built around 1718. It had stables behind it too.

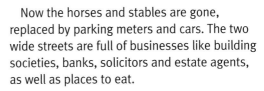

Now the horses and stables are gone, replaced by parking meters and cars. The two wide streets are full of businesses like building societies, banks, solicitors and estate agents, as well as places to eat.

Hide Hill hidden treasure
Early in 1821, when workmen were taking rubbish away from a cabinetmaker's on Hide Hill, they found a small wooden box. Inside were 18 gold coins and 20 silver coins. They were from the reigns of King Henry VIII and his daughters, Queen Mary I and Queen Elizabeth I, so they were 200 to 300 years old when they were found.

What did the workmen do with their unexpected treasure? They sold the coins to a jeweller and spent the money, it's said, on drink. Finders keepers in those days.

Quick Quiz answer (a) eat it. Berwick cockles are a mint-flavoured boiled sweet in the shape of a cockle shell. They are made by William Cowe & Son, of Bridge Street.

Stagecoaches

Because Berwick was on the main road from London to Edinburgh, it was a stopping place for stagecoaches and mail coaches.

The largest was a stagecoach, usually pulled by four horses. This is the kind you see on Christmas cards. In the picture, lanterns shine on the snow and smiling faces look out from the coach windows. The real journey may not have been so jolly.

A Christmas Calamity

Just before Christmas in 1836, frost and heavy snow hit the north-east of England. Strong winds piled the snow into deep drifts, blocking the roads. The stagecoach left Newcastle for Edinburgh at 8 o'clock on the morning of Monday 23 December. It reached Edinburgh at 10 o'clock at night on Thursday 26 December. The journey had taken four days and three nights. Christmas was over.

Passengers leaving the coach at Berwick may have arrived just in time for Christmas. They were probably too cold and tired to enjoy it.

Carriers' Carts

Two hundred years ago there were up to 14 public houses in Sandgate and Hide Hill, and the two streets put together are not very long. The Brown Bear Inn is still on Hide Hill.

The carriers used the public houses as their headquarters. Every week their carts and wagons crisscrossed the roads of the north-east as they collected and delivered goods. This part of town was one of the busiest for trade – and one of the busiest for selling food and drink.

Loads were carried to Belford and Holy Island, to Border towns such as Kelso, Lauder and Coldstream, and on longer journeys to Carlisle and Dumfries.

The hardworking carrier to Newcastle had only one day off a week. His wagon left Berwick at 6 o'clock on a Wednesday morning and he got home again the next Monday evening. Tuesday would be his one day off.

The Pier and Lighthouse

Quick Quiz Who was Grace Darling and
what did she do? *Answer on page 42.*

As soon as you turn into **Ness Street** you can
see the low arch of Pier Gate and the start of
Pier Road. The first houses on Pier Road are
three storeys high with steep gardens behind
them. At the top of the gardens there's a short
length of the old Edwardian Wall and the
curving Black Watch Tower. It's the only
Edwardian tower left standing. The houses
overlook the estuary, where the River Tweed
and the sea meet. The address is Longstone
View, a link with the story of Grace Darling.

Pier Road

There are no safety railings on Pier Road. At
high tide the water laps up to the foot of the
road. When the tide is out it uncovers a flat
stretch of rocks, dark seaweed and pools. This
is the Calot Shad, the shallow place. Building
Pier Road gave work to unemployed men in
Berwick at a time when work was scarce.

The Pier

This is the third pier – they have been built
about 300 years apart, in the 13th century, the
16th and the 19th. The second pier was in ruins
before this one was built. The day the
foundation stone was laid (27 July 1810) was a
noisy one. It began early, with church bells
ringing. Then there was a procession and a
band playing. The day ended with the guns on
the Walls firing in celebration.

Pier fact file

- The pier took 11 years to build, from 1810 to 1821.

- It's built from huge blocks of sandstone cut from cliffs at Scremerston, 4km to the south.

- Berwick Pier is a breakwater, a strong wall built out to sea to give some protection from the north wind.

- Ships didn't tie up at the pier. They docked in the harbour where there is more shelter.

On a fine day it's a pleasant walk along the pier to the lighthouse. You may see grey seals hunting for fish as well as swans feeding. If you're really lucky you may glimpse dolphins out at sea.

The Lighthouse –
'the first and last in England'

The small, dumpy lighthouse sits at the open end of the curving pier. It's red and white, with a red pointed top. When it was built, in 1826, the lantern burnt oil. It was looked after by a lighthouse keeper who lived there with his family. Later the family lived in Pier House and the lighthouse keeper stayed in the lighthouse when he was on duty.

No one lives in the lighthouse now. The lantern is lit by electricity, operated from batteries.

It switches itself on at dusk and off when daylight begins. The light can be seen for over 19km/12 miles. It warns ships of dangers like rocks and shallow water. Berwick harbour has both.

Every lighthouse has a different pattern of lights. Sailors know where they are by reading the lights, like reading road signs on land. The Berwick light is white, flashing out to sea every five seconds.

Quick Quiz answer Grace Darling lived in the Longstone Lighthouse, on one of the Farne Islands. Her father was the lighthouse keeper. One stormy night in September 1838 they rowed out from the lighthouse to rescue the nine survivors of a shipwreck. They were clinging to a rock, surrounded by raging seas. All nine were saved and Grace became famous. She's buried in Bamburgh churchyard and there's a museum close by.

The small open rowing boat the Darlings used was a coble, built at Tweedmouth, across the river from Berwick.

The Palace and Lower Town

Quick Quiz Was there oil in **Oil Mill Lane**? *Answer on page 45.*

This part of Berwick is close to the harbour, so it is the lowest part of town. But if you're looking for a fairy-tale palace with towers and turrets and flags flying, you won't find one. The Scottish kings may have lived in this part of town, but the Palace name belongs to the Governor's House. It was the grandest building in Berwick when it was built in 1719 for the military governor to live in.

The Palace or Governor's House

The house is in Palace Street East. It was built with storehouses, a bakehouse and a brewhouse in the grounds. The large garden was noted for its rich soil. Outside the walls were tall trees with a rowdy rookery of birds and nests. To find the Governor's House, look for one with a small stone-built porch at the front, with a window and a curved roof. Above it is a white-painted coat of arms.

The Lower Town

There are two streets and a square with 'Palace' in their names and they're all linked. **Palace Street East** is where the Governor's

House is. The quiet square is **Palace Green**.
Behind the Palace Green houses is **Palace
Street**.

Palace Green has a green in the centre, with a
low wall and railings round it. The green used
to be a bowling green. The statue of Jimmy
Strength stood here.

Palace Street is where the shipbuilder Arthur
Byram lived, at number 25. There's a stone
above the door carved with his initials, AB, and
the date, 1782. Byram's business on the
quayside was very successful. New boats were
launched down the slipway into the River
Tweed.

The Main Guard, with its pillared front, is on
the corner of Palace Green and Palace Street,
close to the Walls. The story of the Main Guard
is on page 81.

At the other end of Palace Street is **Foul Ford**.
It's an odd name but this probably was a smelly
part of the Lower Town. The houses had open
drains, with middens and dung heaps piled
high in the street. Many households kept cattle,
horses or pigs. Heavy rain would flood the open
drains and wash all the smelly rubbish downhill
to lie in the hollow of Foul Ford.

Horses were kept at Campbell's Coach House
and Stables in Foul Ford. The name is still there,
above the arched doors of the old coach house.
From Foul Ford two cobbled lanes lead back to
Palace Street East. The wider one is Oil Mill
Lane. It joins Palace Street East opposite The
Avenue and a long green, which was used as a
ropery.

Money for old rope

Berwick had a workhouse for poor people, where the old men were given tough old rope to untwist as their work. Children helped them after school. The loose fibres, called oakum, were then reused, packed between the planks of wooden boats to keep out the water.

Quick Quiz answer There was oil in Oil Mill Lane but it was an unusual oil mill. It was a linseed crushing mill. Linseed oil comes from the flax plant. The oil was used in oil paint and linoleum and in oil cake for animal feed.

The Tall Tale of Jimmy Strength

- His real name was James Stewart.
- He was born on Christmas Day, 1728.
- He married 5 times and had 27 children.
- He died on 18 April 1844, aged 115 years.

It was James Stewart himself who gave all these facts. He also said that he was born in America, fought with the British army and navy, and was related to the Scottish royal family.

People enjoyed hearing his tall stories but they may not have believed him even then. What was true was his nickname, Jimmy Strength. He was amazingly strong. He could lift a large wooden dining table with his teeth or lift heavy weights fastened to an iron bar using only one hand. Even as an old man he earned a little money by performing acts of strength, and by playing the fiddle. He hated to be called a beggar.

We even have some idea of what Jimmy Strength looked like. A local artist, Thomas Sword Good, painted his picture. Another local artist, James Wilson, made a lifesize statue of him.

In the painting Jimmy Strength looks a bit scary. He's short, with a big head and nose and heavy hunched shoulders. He wears ragged clothes and is playing the fiddle. An upturned top hat lies beside him to collect money.

For the statue, Jimmy Strength had his hat on his head and the fiddle under his arm – although he is holding out his hand for money. He liked the statue because he thought it looked like him.

For a long time the statue stood on Palace Green but only a few pieces are left. There are plans for a new statue.

Marygate, the Town Hall and Berwick's Famous Bells

Quick Quiz Is a carillon (a) a kind of cake or (b) a set of bells? *Answer on page 50.*

Marygate

Marygate begins at the Scotsgate and ends at the town hall. It's one of the main shopping streets. The twice-weekly Charter Market has been held here for hundreds of years. Scotsgate is the oldest Gate through the Walls. The path across the top is on the Elizabethan Walls.

The best view of Marygate and the town hall is from this path. Look for Sidey Court, a plain building on the left, as you look downhill. There's a small badge on the wall, like a bicycle wheel with spokes. You can just make out the letters CTC. They stand for Cyclists' Touring Club. The building was the Avenue Hotel and it welcomed cyclists. The CTC is still used by keen cyclists.

While Scotsgate is a gate, Marygate is the name of the street. It comes from the 12th-century St Mary's Church, pulled down when the Elizabethan Walls were built. This is a place where bones have been found, probably from St Mary's graveyard. The Red Lion coaching inn was in Marygate, where Woolworths is now. It had stables for 66 horses behind the inn. The main public room was big enough to hang three large crystal chandeliers and six smaller ones. Berwick has nothing quite like that today.

Off Marygate, both West Street and Eastern Lane lead to Bridge Street. They are so steep that you gallop down them rather than walk. The Maltings Theatre and Arts Centre on Eastern Lane used to be a granary. It went up in flames in 1984. The inside, with its wooden floors, was burnt out. The strong stone walls survived to be rebuilt as a theatre.

Marygate today

Some Berwick people feel that Marygate was spoilt in the 20th century. A few buildings on one side were pulled down at **Golden Square** for the road leading to the Royal Tweed Bridge. Before that the two unbroken rows of buildings faced each other across a cobbled street.

Marygate is now part of a Conservation Area. There are rules about the kind of new buildings being put up, the style of shop windows and signs, even the colours of paint you should use. When the old bus station on Marygate was pulled down, three shops were built to fill the gap. They fit in so well with the older buildings you may find it difficult to spot them.

The Town Hall or Guildhall

This is where Marygate ends. The town hall was built in the middle of the 18th century – and in the middle of the road. Marygate, Church Street, Woolmarket and Hide Hill all meet at the corner of the town hall. This makes one of Berwick's busiest junctions. Even crossing the street can be difficult.

The first thing you notice about the town hall is the spire. It's 40 metres/150 feet high, topped by a weather vane shaped like an arrow. You can see it from all over town, and from out to sea. Ships use the spire as a marker to enter the harbour.

Below the spire is a clock tower with four faces. The clocks share the same winding mechanism so they do tell the same time. Berwick's eight bells are hung in the bell tower.

The main town hall entrance on Marygate is very grand. It has wide steps, tall pillars and a heavy door. The side entrance, for tourist visitors, is much plainer. There's a copy of the town stocks near it. Three people could be fastened in the stocks by their ankles, often for drunkenness or name-calling. It's a long time since it was used.

When the town hall was built it was used for Guild meetings and for elections. Courts (Quarter Sessions) were held four times a year so the building had cells to hold the prisoners. Now it's used for official occasions and for events like sales of work, coffee mornings and dinner dances.

Summer tours of the town hall start in the long room on the first floor. The new smooth wooden floor has been laid on top of worn flagstones. Tables wobbled, drinks were spilt and dancers tripped up on the old uneven floor. The new floor isn't fixed so it can be lifted again.

Go straight to gaol

The gaol on the upper floor was a fearful place. The cell windows still have their iron bars. The cell doors are thick and heavy. Iron keys, latches, bars and chains are so heavy you can hardly lift them, although you can try. There's a condemned cell with no window and hidden iron bars built into the walls. There was no escape.

The last person to use the condemned cell was Grace Griffin. In 1823 she spent her final lonely hours here before being taken to Gallows Hill, near the present railway station.

To pass the time, some prisoners carved their names on the cell walls. Sailors (maybe in overnight for drunkenness) drew ships with sails. The names and drawings are still there.

Quick Quiz answer (b) a carillon is a set of bells that can be played together. They're usually hung in a tower, like the Berwick bells.

Berwick's Famous Bells

In January of 1998, two of Berwick's famous bells were smashed to bits with hammers. It wasn't an accident. The bells were cracked and had to be broken up in the bell tower of the town hall before they could be taken away.

All eight bells were rehung in time for the Millennium New Year, ringing out a full peal at midnight on 31 December 1999.

It cost £66,000 to repair the bells and strengthen the bell tower. About 250 years earlier the bells were sent to London to be recast, so they were not new in 1754. That repair cost £353.

Each bell has a number, and a name linking it with the town.

1. **James Stuart,** after Berwick's strongman, 'Jimmy Strength'.

2. **Philip,** after a local Victorian doctor, Philip Whiteside Maclagen.

3. **Joseph,** after Joseph Weatherston, a mayor of Berwick in the 1890s.

4. **William,** after William Temple, mayor when this town hall was built.

5. **Fenwick,** after Colonel George Fenwick, a Governor of Berwick in the 17th century.

6. **Cuthbert,** after St Cuthbert, the famous northern saint and a bishop of Lindisfarne (Holy Island).

7. **Elizabeth** is named after Queen Elizabeth II, who has visited Berwick.

8. **King James,** after the king who united the crowns of Scotland and England. He was welcomed to Berwick in 1603 on his way to be crowned in London.

Cuthbert and Elizabeth were the bells broken with hammers. Two bells from Worcestershire, which weren't needed there, have replaced them.

Fenwick was also replaced, but the old Fenwick bell has been kept. It's the Curfew Bell. It still rings the curfew for 15 minutes at 8 o'clock at night (not Sundays), a reminder of the days when everyone had to be indoors by then.

While the bells were being repaired the bellringers practised in Bamburgh Parish Church, ready to ring all eight bells to welcome in the new millennium.

Church and Chapel and Stories from the Graveyard

Quick Quiz Is a millennium a hundred years or a thousand years? *Answer on page 55.*

Church and Chapel

From behind the town hall, Church Street climbs uphill to the parish church of Holy Trinity and St Mary. The St Mary name was added in 1989 when St Mary's at the top of Castlegate was closed.

Berwick used to have churches, chapels and religious meeting houses in almost every street. Just over 100 years ago there were 14 – English, Scottish and Catholic churches, Baptist and Methodist chapels and the Salvation Army.

These four are on Church Street and the Parade:

1. In Chapel Street, off Church Street, is the **Middle Meeting House**, a chapel which is now a warehouse.

2. **St Aidan's**, now the Peace Church, is at the end of a row of houses behind the main street. Other churches and chapels were hidden away like this. Church Street, Marygate and Ravensdowne all have these passageways. They were built on when Berwick was short of land for housing.

3. **Wallace Green Church of Scotland** is at the top of Church Street.

4. **Holy Trinity Church** is tucked away across the open stretch of Parade. In summer it's almost hidden by trees.

Holy Trinity – A Very Special Church

Holy Trinity fact file

1. It was built between 1650 and 1652. Some of the stone was taken from Berwick castle, which was already falling down.

2. It was built when the country had neither a king nor a queen but was a Commonwealth. The ruler was Oliver Cromwell. The king, Charles I, had lost his head in 1649.

3. This is the only Commonwealth church in the north of England.

4. Oliver Cromwell was a Puritan. Puritans wanted churches and services to be pure – that meant plain and simple. So Holy Trinity had no tower, no bells ('a useless tinkling of brass and iron,' said Cromwell), no organ for church music, no altar, no font for baptisms, and no stained-glass windows.

The church has all of these now except a tower. It had no bell until 1951. Before that a bell in the town hall was rung before church services. Sometimes visitors thought the town hall was the church and hammered on the door to get in.

Four things to see in Holy Trinity:

1. **Large.** The colourful stained-glass window above the entrance door. The Borough coat of arms is near the foot of the centre panel. The colours are brightest when the sun shines from the west.

2. **Small.** The dark wood memorial to Colonel George Fenwick, in the right-hand aisle underneath the crossed flags. His story is told on pages 78–79.

3. **Old.** Against the bottom wall of the same aisle is a wooden chest with carved panels. It came from the much older chapel of Berwick castle. A table from Cromwell's time is in front of it.

4. **New.** The Millennium Window, on the left wall, dates from 2000. The side panels show the two northern saints, Columba and Aidan. The centre panel shows Holy Trinity Church and the Tree of Life, and then the Water of Life, a symbol here for the River Tweed.

Quick Quiz answer A millennium is a thousand years. A hundred years is a century.

Stories from the Graveyard

Holy Trinity churchyard is crowded with tombstones of different kinds. Among them are 'table' tombs with a flat top, like a table. Other headstones have sunk into the ground and others are worn smooth by wind and rain.

There are still some you can read. They can give names and ages, maybe where the person lived and their occupation. Because Berwick was a port, you'll find a Shipbuilder, a Master Mariner and a Supervisor of Excise buried here.

This is written on one headstone: To the Memory of Thomas Todd who with manly integrity served the office of Treasurer of this Corporation for 34 years. Died 1805 aged 73.

Robbing and rioting

More than 200 years ago newly dug graves were being robbed in Berwick. A young woman and a child were dug up shortly after burial and the bodies disappeared. Rumours flew around the town that three young surgeons were to blame.

An angry crowd gathered outside the house of one of them, Robert Nesbitt. They became so angry that they knocked down a building. Bodies were found inside. Robert Nesbitt fled.

The crowd moved to another property and became more unruly. This was serious. The police called in a magistrate and he read the Riot Act to them. This meant the crowd had to leave within an hour. When they didn't, troops had to be called out. This was a rare and dangerous situation in Berwick.

A reward was offered for the capture of Robert Nesbitt. The other two surgeons were arrested and tried in court. The verdict? Not guilty.

Yew trees and time capsules

In a quiet corner of the churchyard, near the parish hall, are two tiny trees with a low fence round each. They were planted to celebrate the millennium (the year 2000), and they're cuttings from 2,000-year-old Welsh yew trees. The Tennant Melangel Yew was planted by Holy Trinity First School. The Ffynnon Bedr Yew was planted by St Mary's First School.

Buried under the trees in the churchyard are two time capsules, put there by the school children. Inside each are pictures of all the children with examples of their work, and the names of everyone at the schools – pupils, teaching staff, caretakers, cleaning and dinner staff, and the school governors.

When time capsules are buried they're meant to be discovered some time in the future. Perhaps in a hundred years time, or even in a thousand years, someone will dig them up again.

Wallace Green, the Parade, the Barracks and the Town Waits

Quick Quiz 1. Did a Mr Wallace live at Wallace Green? 2. Did soldiers parade on the Parade? *The answers are in this chapter.*

Wallace Green

Wallace Green is a short, wide street, from Wallace Green Church to the Walls. It's an odd name as there's no Green now and there wasn't a Mr Wallace. The name is from Walls Green, the Green by the Walls.

Two important buildings on Wallace Green

1. **Wallace Green Church of Scotland** was built in 1858, with seats for up to a thousand people. The 38-metre spire is almost as tall as the town hall spire.

2. **The Borough Council Offices** have the town coat of arms on the wall, with two trees and two bears, one bear sitting and one standing. It also has 13 tall chimneys which are not used now.

The Council offices were originally built as a gaol to replace the town hall gaol. A few prisoners escaped from the town hall, which wasn't surprising. They were left alone for most of the day. The gaoler only visited three times a day. The new gaol was more secure. It had 16 cells and the gaoler and his family lived there too. There was also a man called a turnkey. He kept the keys of the gaol and was really a prison warder. Both men and women were held in Berwick gaol.

After only 40 years it was closed as a gaol. The cells are still used – some for storage, but staff use others as *very* small offices.

The Parade

The name is at least 300 years old so it's older than the army barracks beside it. Soldiers did sometimes use it as a parade ground. It has never been built on but has been used as a town rubbish dump (which included heaps of horse dung), and tennis courts. In the Second World War the army covered it with wooden huts. Now it's used as a car park.

The Barracks, a First in Britain

Berwick Barracks were the first in the country specially built to house soldiers. Before that Berwick soldiers had to live in ale houses. When these were full they were boarded in private houses. The owners complained that they weren't paid on time, and the soldiers complained that their rooms were cold and damp.

After years of complaints the barracks were built. Then there was no money left to furnish them. The town quickly raised some money and the soldiers moved in. It was July 1721, and there was room for 600 men and 36 officers.

Since then the barracks have been altered and added to but the army used them until 1964. It was the headquarters of the King's Own Scottish Borderers from 1881 to 1964.

Now the buildings are open as three

museums. The English Heritage 'By Beat of
Drum' shows you what a soldier's life was like,
with lifesize models and colourful uniforms,
weapons and medals. The Clock Block (it does
have a clock above the door) is the Borough
Museum, with 'A Window on Berwick' and the
town's Burrell Collection. There's more about Sir
William Burrell on page 79.

Quick Quiz anwers, in case you didn't find
them. 1. No, the name is from Walls Green. 2.
Yes, soldiers did parade there.

The Town Waits

The Waits weren't waiting for anything. It's an old name for a group of musicians who played in the streets. The Berwick Waits played on special occasions. They led processions to and from church on Christmas Day and when a new mayor was elected, and they played for important visitors to the town.

The ideal number of Waits was four because then they could play as a quartet. They weren't paid much – only £8 a year. At one time they had to share £6 so they earned extra money by teaching music and playing at private dinners.

All the musicians were professional players. They could lose their position as a Wait if they didn't play to a high standard.

Their official uniform was a heavy blue cloak with gold bands. It was long and wrapped round them to keep out the cold. They also wore a large hat with gold bands. They probably enjoyed parading the streets wearing this grand uniform. Everyone would look at them.

Because they marched and played at the same time, their instruments had to be easy to carry. These were usually stringed instruments, like violins or violas, or the deeper-sounding oboe.

As the years went on the Waits were asked to play less often. They were paid 75p/15 shillings to play for the Duke of Cumberland when he visited Berwick in 1771. The story goes that the Duke was glad to leave the town – and the music – behind him.

But local people couldn't escape so easily. Before Christmas it was the habit of the Waits to play in the streets while the people were asleep. Perhaps no one missed them too much when it all came to an end early in the 19th century.

The last of the Town Waits lived until 1854. He was a blind fiddler called James Wallace.

Castlegate, the Castle and the Railway Station

Quick Quiz See number 4 in 'Four to find on Castlegate' for the quick quiz about a swan. *Answer on page 65.*

Castlegate

Castlegate is the long street that starts at the Scotsgate, just outside the safety of the Elizabethan Walls. It led to Berwick Castle and the main road north and to Scotland. Castlegate was inside the earlier Edwardian Walls so it was a safer place then.

Four to find on Castlegate

1. Queen Victoria's Diamond Jubilee **drinking fountain** (1897) is at the start of Castlegate.

2. Across the road is the old **cattle market,** now Berwick's main car park. It's built on the moat that lay at the foot of the Elizabethan Wall. The cattle market was moved here from the open streets in 1886. This is a good place to look up at the height of the Wall and imagine how difficult it would be for an attacker to reach the top.

3. The **war memorial** at the top of Castlegate, with a bronze winged figure on top.

4. Along Railway Street and facing the railway station there's a **swan** that never flies away. Can you find it? Keep looking up. *Answer on page 65.*

Berwick Castle

Berwick Castle had a long history, from the 12th century to the 19th. It was the scene of royal visits and great feasts, but it was once captured by seven Scots. They dug their way into the castle and then let in another 40 men.

The castle was built on high ground looking down on the river. Towers, gates, drawbridges and ditches protected it – until guns replaced arrows and spears. The first time guns were used, the castle garrison took fright and surrendered at once.

From the station platform you can see the remains of a castle wall across the railway lines. From the station car park a path leads down into Castle Vale Park. This path is beside the castle's Constable Tower. The Tower is on private land but it's easy to see from the park path.

The rest is best seen from the riverside walk, the **New Road,** which runs under the railway bridge. (It's not new now. It was built in 1816, but it's still called Berwick's New Road.)

Three Castle Survivors, seen from the New Road. The first two were begun by Edward I and the third in the time of Henry VIII.

1. **The White Wall,** which drops in a jagged line from the castle to the river. Skeletons and bones were found beside the White Wall when the railway station was being built. They may be burials of soldiers from the castle.

2. **The Breakyneck Steps,** which were protected by the White Wall. They were built as a safe way between castle and river. They're not safe now and can't be used. You can see why they are called Breakyneck – one slip and you could break your neck.

3. **The Water Tower** or **White Wall Tower,** at the river's edge. The circular tower was added in the 16th century. On the New Road you walk right through the ruins.

The Castle was fought over as often as the town. It was won and lost by both England and Scotland. It was robbed of stone to build Holy Trinity church and the barracks. Later, parts of it fell down. When the North British Railway Company bought the castle it was a ruin, and they blew up what was left to build the railway station.

Quick Quiz answer Find the swan. The stone swan is carved above the upper window of a building which used to be the Black Swan Hotel (beside number 16 Railway Street).

The Railway Station

The Victorians built the first railway station, and they built it to look like a castle with towers, turrets and battlements. It's been rebuilt and doesn't look like a castle now.

How the railway came to Berwick

1846 The railway from Edinburgh reached Berwick, but it stopped there. Because the passengers had crossed from Scotland into England, Customs and Excise men were waiting on Berwick platform. Passengers were shocked to find that anyone carrying Scotch whisky had to pay duty on it.

1847 The railway from Newcastle reached Tweedmouth, but it stopped there. There was no rail bridge across the River Tweed. Passengers had to cross the Old Bridge in a horse-drawn coach on the way to

Berwick station. Cattle were driven on foot from Tweedmouth station to Berwick station. The station had loading bays for cattle and horses. Animals often travelled by rail.

1850 The Royal Border Bridge was opened. Passengers could travel from Edinburgh to London without changing trains. While the bridge was being built, the go-ahead railway company arranged day trips to Berwick so that passengers could see the work going on.

It wasn't only passengers and animals that travelled by rail. Market trains ran from Berwick to other cities and towns, carrying fresh produce from Border farms. One train left Berwick at 4.30 a.m. and arrived in Edinburgh at 7.15 a.m. The goods were delivered to the fruit and vegetable market in Market Street, behind the main railway station. They would be in the shops for opening time that morning.

As soon as the railway came to Berwick, stagecoaches stopped their journeys and the horses were put up for sale. Soon, the shipping companies cut back on their journeys too. But the railway brought lots of other work to Berwick. You can find out what these jobs were in the chapter Earning a Living.

The Greenses

Quick Quiz The Bell Tower is octagonal in shape. How many sides does it have? *Answer on page 69.*

The Greenses

This is the local name for **Low Greens** and **High Greens**. Together they're called the Greenses. They were kept green so there was a clear view from the castle to the sea and north to Scotland. Buildings would have blocked the view and got in the line of fire. This was just another hazard of living in a frontier town.

The Early Greenses – two to see

1. **The Bell Tower,** built about 1577. This is an Elizabethan watchtower in a super position overlooking the sea, the fields and the town. There are ruins of the Edwardian Walls near it. The Bell Tower had a bell which would be rung to warn of danger. At one time there was a beacon on top as well. It was one of a chain of beacons along the coast. They would be lit if the country was invaded – an early warning system of the time.

   Other towers also protected the Greenses. They included the **Damned Tower, Murderer Tower** and **Red Tower**.

2. **Lord's Mount,** built about 1540. It's near the Bell Tower, and was a Henry VIII artillery fort. For over 400 years it was hidden under earth and rubble. What you see now was uncovered in the 1970s. You can walk round the ground floor and see fireplaces, a bread oven and a privy.

Victorian Greenses – the growing years

Victoria was Queen from 1837 to 1901. The Greenses grew into a busy fishing community during this time, with its own harbour. There were fishermen at almost every address. In one house the father was a fisherman, and three of the sons, aged 24, 21 and 16, were also fishermen.

Three Victorian buildings

1. The Greenses had its own church, St Mary's, built 1857–8 and closed in 1989.

2. The Greenses had its own school from 1866. It was used for more than 100 years.

3. Berwick Infirmary moved to Low Greens in 1874 and is still there.

Close to the infirmary is a memorial to Dr Philip Maclagan, a well-loved local doctor. He died in 1892. The figure is Hygeia, the goddess of health.

Early years in the Greenses – pigs, geese and poisonous weeds

Not everyone in the early Greenses was a good neighbour. Many families kept pigs, and in High Greens these sometimes roamed the streets, 'to the annoyance of the neighbours'. Wandering geese were a problem too. And there were grumbles that High Greens was so full of thistles and poisonous weeds that grazing cattle were in danger from eating them.

Later years in the Greenses – bathing pools and workhouse rules

In the last century the Greenses had two open-air bathing ponds at Greens Haven. The large one was for gentlemen and had spaces for indoor or outdoor dressing. The smaller one was for ladies. It was a suitable distance from the men's pond and had a shelter for bathers. Swimmers must have been tough. They swam in unheated sea water with no real protection from the weather.

The Berwick Workhouse was in High Greens. The very name terrified people. They knew if there was no work there was no money. If there was no money, they could be sent to the workhouse. About 150 years ago, more than 150 men, women and children were staying there.

It was run by the parish, so poor people did have somewhere to stay. You did unpaid work in return for your bed and board – and you were listed as 'pauper'. Your whole day was governed by workhouse rules.

- Get up at 5 a.m. in summer and 7 a.m. in winter.
- Go to bed at 9 p.m. in summer and 8 p.m. in winter.
- Attend church twice on Sunday.
- Change your clothes once a week, on a Sunday.
- Change your bedding once a month, but search for vermin twice a week.

Quick Quiz answer The octagonal Bell Tower has eight sides.

The Boggy Battle of Halidon Hill

Where? It was fought just north of Berwick, on and around Halidon Hill.

When? 19 July 1333.

Why? It was yet another border battle between England (under King Edward III) and Scotland (led by Sir Archibald Douglas). Berwick was a Scottish town in 1333.

Before the battle

The English army took up position on top of Halidon Hill, looking down on Berwick and the Scots. Before the battle began the Scots challenged the English to a duel. This would be a single combat, to the death, between their champion, the chief of the Turnbull clan, and any knight in the English army.

The duel

No one really wanted to fight Turnbull. He was a giant of a man and as strong as a bull. What was worse, he had a gigantic black dog with him. At last a young English knight, Sir Robert Benhale, took up the challenge. He was much slimmer and weaker-looking than Turnbull.

At once, Turnbull let loose his dog and it rushed straight at Benhale. Moving swiftly aside, Benhale swung at the dog and killed it with a single blow of his sword. Then the two men began a long and savage fight. Although Turnbull had the strength, Benhale had the speed. Finally, Turnbull was killed. The Scotsman's head was described as 'rolling upon the heather'.

The battle

Having lost the duel, the Scottish army began their advance on Halidon Hill. Although the ground between the two armies looked solid it was marshy. As the Scots tramped across it, men and horses sank into the boggy ground.

Then the steel-tipped arrows of the English longbowmen showered down on them and many were killed. As the survivors began to climb Halidon Hill, the English soldiers rolled rocks down upon them. The Scots had to break ranks to escape.

Some began to run away. Others stayed and were cut down by English swords in hand-to-hand fighting. Scenting victory, the English chased after the Scots, sometimes as far as the sea. There, many drowned.

The slaughter was terrible. Douglas, the Scots leader, was one who lost his life, along with earls, knights and thousands of foot soldiers. This was a battle won by King Edward III of England. But it was not the final battle fought over the wild frontier town of Berwick upon Tweed.

The battlesite today

A tourist viewpoint, illustrated panels and parking can be reached from a minor road (signposted) off the Duns Road, the A6105, not far from the A1 bypass road at the north end of Berwick. Although the marshy ground has been drained, you can still imagine what the battlefield was like in 1333 – the advantage Halidon Hill gave to the English army, even the distance the Scots fled before they reached the sea.

Earning a Living

Quick Quiz Two hundred years ago there were huckster shops in Berwick. Did a huckster sell (a) small articles that were easily carried or (b) corn and other feed for animals? *Answer on page 76.*

200 Years Ago – The Butcher, the Baker, the Candlestick Maker

Two hundred years ago you could buy everything you needed in the Berwick shops and markets. There were butchers and there were bakers, including special biscuit and gingerbread bakers. There were grocers, confectioners and tobacconists. There were stationers and booksellers, shoemakers, hatters, drapers and wine shops.

There were no candlestick makers in Berwick but there were tallow chandlers – shops where candles were made or sold. These would be bestsellers. When it was dark, the only light indoors came from candles or a coal fire.

Ironmongers and china shops may have sold candlesticks. Blacksmiths and tinsmiths may have made them.

There was a man in Berwick called Mr Berwick. He was a barber.

Odd jobs

Would you rather:

Be a gaoler or a pawnbroker?

Weave stockings or make clogs?

Be a cow and horse doctor, or a farrier (shoe horses)?

One woman earned a living from her mangle. This had heavy wooden rollers and a handle. People took their clean, wet washing to her and it would be fed through the rollers as the handle was turned. This squeezed out some of the water, more than you could wring out by hand.

Berwick had a few bakehouses in the busier streets. The bakehouse owner would cook food you'd made at home but couldn't cook over an open fire. Many houses had no oven so you used the bakehouse. Like the woman with the mangle, the bakehouse owner charged for this service.

The overseer of the street scavengers or cleaners had a good job. He would never be out of work.

100 Years Ago – Wheels

By 1850 the railway had arrived in Berwick. Over the years it brought more jobs to the town than you would ever guess.

Engine drivers and firemen were important people in the days of steam engines. But the railways also needed guards for goods trains and passenger trains, signalmen in the signal boxes, platelayers who worked on the railway tracks. The steam engines needed cleaners, fitters and boiler men.

The passenger station needed clerks, porters and ticket inspectors. Berwick had a 'Keeper of the Refreshment Rooms'. There was even a railway detective living in the town, as well as a steam-engine maker.

Next to the passenger station was a goods yard, also engine sheds, a coal store and a grain store. It was one of the busiest, noisiest and dirtiest places in Berwick.

Many of the railway workers lived in the Greenses, close to their work. Between 80 and 100 people earned a living working for the railways.

Odd jobs

Would you rather:

Make false teeth or straw hats?

Keep an old-clothes shop or dig graves?

Make sausage skins, or dress tripe (that meant cleaning the stomach lining of an ox or cow before it was cooked and eaten)?

The man with the longest job title in Berwick was the 'Sanitary Inspector for dairies and cowsheds and common lodging houses and superintendent at the cattle market'.

Berwick had a father and son who both taught music. The father was an organist and the son was a violinist.

This was the time of Cycling Clubs, a new hobby mainly for men. Both Tweedmouth and Berwick had Cycling Clubs. There was a man in Berwick who earned a living making bicycle wheels.

Quick Quiz answer A huckster sold (a) small articles like combs, pins and ribbons, either in a shop or carried in the street to sell.

Four People – the Painter, the Writer, the Soldier, and the Collector Who Lived in a Castle

Quick Quiz Which of the four people in this chapter links America and the Coldstream Guards with Berwick? Take a guess, then find out if you're right when you're reading the chapter. *Answer on page 80.*

The Painter. L.S. Lowry and his 'matchstick' men

L.S. Lowry (1887–1976) was the artist who painted dark pictures of smoking chimneys, factories, and narrow streets filled with small black figures – his 'matchstick' men.

But Lowry also loved the sea, and he loved Berwick. He spent many holidays in the town painting pictures of the town hall, the High Street, Quay Walls and Bridge End.

One of his brighter paintings was of a beach shelter close to Berwick Pier. A few years ago this was uncared for and was going to be pulled down. A plan was made to repair it and it has been saved. It's now called the Lowry shelter.

Lowry's paintings fetch very high prices now. A painting of Berwick might cost up to £300,000. When he was in Berwick, Lowry stayed at the Castle Hotel, close to the railway station. He made sketches of one of the staff but she didn't keep any of them.

The Writer. Charles Dickens (1812–1870)

You may think that a writer travelling around the country to read from his work is something new. It's not. Charles Dickens did it about 150 years ago.

He visited Berwick twice to give readings. A plaque on the wall of the King's Arms Hotel on Hide Hill gives the dates he stayed there.

His books are long but he wrote them to be read in shorter sections, often in monthly magazines. Like today's TV 'soaps', each episode ended when something exciting or tragic was going to happen. Readers looked forward to the next part of the story.

Many of his stories are still used today in the theatre and cinema, and on television and radio. He chose interesting or amusing names for his characters, like Scrooge the miser, the kindly Mr Pickwick and the boy, Oliver Twist, who asked for more to eat.

When Charles Dickens was 10, his father was put in prison for debt. Dickens was so afraid of owing money that he never stopped working. He was famous at 25, but died when he was only 58.

The Soldier. Colonel George Fenwick

What links America and the Coldstream Guards with Berwick? The answer is Colonel George Fenwick.

High on a wall in Holy Trinity Church are two crossed flags. Below them is a dark wood memorial. The flags belonged to the Coldstream Guards and the memorial is to Colonel Fenwick. He died in 1656.

- **The Colonel.** He was a friend of the Puritan leader Oliver Cromwell and he became Governor of Berwick when Cromwell was in power. The Colonel also helped to raise money to build the present Holy Trinity Church.
- **America.** Earlier in his life, Fenwick was the second Governor of the Saybrook Colony, in Connecticut, America. The Puritans owned the land there.
- **Coldstream Guards.** When he was in Berwick, the Colonel raised five companies of men for the newly formed Coldstream Guards. The flags hanging in the church are the old colours of the regiment. They were laid up in the church in the year 2000. That's the year Holy Trinity and the Coldstream Guards had their 350th anniversaries. Colonel Fenwick saw the beginning of them both.

The Collector. Sir William Burrell and the Berwick Collection

William Burrell (1861–1958) was a Scottish shipowner and art collector. At one time he lived at Hutton Castle, close to Berwick. That's how the town had a Burrell Collection a long time before the big Burrell Collection in Glasgow.

There's a story that William Burrell would call in at the old museum in the High Street and hand over small treasures pulled from his pocket. The museum curator thinks this is just a story.

What is true is that the art gallery and museum, now in Berwick Barracks, has 42 paintings he gave them, including *Russian Dancers* by Degas. William Burrell was fussy about his paintings. He had the last word on where and how they were hung in the old museum.

He gave Berwick hundreds of other items as well, such as pieces of his favourite blue and white Chinese porcelain. Some of them are on show in the museum too.

Quick Quiz answer Colonel George Fenwick is the link.

Four Places – Main Guard, Gunpowder Magazine, Lions House, Ice Houses

Quick Quiz Was it hot work or cold work filling the ice houses with ice? *Answer in the Ice Houses section and on page 84.*

The Main Guard

How old is it? It dates from the 18th century.

Where is it? On the corner of Palace Green and Palace Street, close to the Walls.

There were four guard houses in Berwick, built to guard the town gates. The Main Guard is the only one left. It was moved from Marygate in 1815 and rebuilt stone by stone. Soldiers from the barracks used the guard houses when they were on duty.

The Main Guard has two rooms, with a cell called the black hole between them. The cell has no windows so it is always dark. Prisoners, often drunk and rowdy, were locked inside until they were sober. The bigger of the two rooms was for the soldiers on guard. They had wooden benches to lie on and a fire to keep them warm. The smaller room was for the officer of the guard. The building has a deep open porch (a portico), and pillars at the front.

The Main Guard (English Heritage) is now a Heritage Centre, run by Berwick Civic Society. There are two displays inside, and one of them is usually changed each year.

The Gunpowder Magazine

How old is it? It was built in 1749.
Where is it? It faces the Walls, between Windmill Bastion and King's Mount.

Before this Gunpowder Magazine was built, the army stored explosives at Brass Bastion, nearer the barracks. When there was a threat to Berwick from Bonnie Prince Charlie and his Scottish troops, the gunpowder store was checked. The gunpowder was damp and useless. A new and better magazine had to be built.

The builders took no chances with this one. The stone walls are very strong. There are no windows. The door faces the sea, away from the town. The roof is double, to give ventilation and strength.

The builders even used wooden pegs instead of iron nails. Soldiers couldn't wear hobnailed boots inside the magazine. Iron could have caused sparks and set fire to the gunpowder. This magazine kept the gunpowder dry, and there never was an explosion.

Lions House

How old is it? About 200 years old (built in 1809).
Where is it? It's a short way behind the Gunpowder Magazine.

Lions House is a plain grey three-storey house. It's been built on one of the windiest places in Berwick, and close to the older gunpowder magazine.

The house looks like a child's drawing. On the ground floor are four windows with a door right in the middle. There are five windows on the first floor and on the second floor. The plain roof has chimney pots at each end.

The name tells you what is special about the house. Two stone lions guard the entrance gate. Their eyes are wide open and so are their mouths, showing wicked teeth.

The Lions House gardens are now neat allotments, sheltered in a hollow from the sea winds. Healthy fruit bushes, flowers, potatoes and beans grow well in the dark soil.

Ice Houses

How old are they? The three that survive are about 200 years old.

Where are they?

1. Between the Lions House and Ravensdowne. Look for a high wall crowned with ivy.
2. At the foot of Bankhill, under the Royal Tweed Bridge. Look for low wooden doors.
3. At Shoregate, next to the Customs House parking space. This may be open once a year on Doors Open Day, a Saturday in September.

What were they for? Berwick salmon was packed in crushed ice before travelling south by sea. The ice came from local ponds and was stored in the ice houses until it was needed. If the winter was mild, extra ice was brought to Berwick from Scandinavia. It had to be paid for.

The ice houses needed thick stone walls to keep the cold in and the warmth out. The floor sloped so that melting ice could drain away. There was often an opening near the roof to shovel in the ice. Ice is heavy so this was hot work.

   The Shoregate ice house was the biggest. It's high, with a domed roof and sloping floor. It's cold inside even on a sunny day.

A cold meal
In January 1814 the River Tweed froze. Fifty Berwick gentlemen pitched a tent on the ice then sat inside and ate dinner. This had happened before, about 70 years earlier. Perhaps the winters really were colder in the 18th and 19th centuries.

   Quick Quiz answer in case you missed it. It's hot work because ice is heavy.

Twenty Questions

1. Which tall king was
   nicknamed 'Longshanks'?

2. On the Borough coat of arms, which animal
   is chained to a tree?

3. What kind of swans will you find in Berwick?

4. How long did it take to build the Old Bridge
   – over 14 years or over 24 years?

5. Who is the lady with the dogs?

6. How many gun platforms are there on the
   Eight Gun Battery?

7. What did egglers collect?

8. What's the name of the spooky place just off the Quayside?

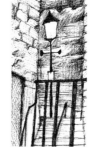

9. What did Grace Darling do?

10. What was the nickname of James Stewart, Berwick's strongman?

11. What are Philip, Joseph and Fenwick the names of?

12. Where will you find a millennium window and two tiny yew trees?

13. What did a turnkey do?

14. Is the New Road new?

15. How many Greens are there in the Greenses?

16. What happened to Turnbull at the Battle of Halidon Hill?

17. What did a farrier do?

18. What did a tripe dresser do?

19. Who wrote about Scrooge the miser, and the hungry boy Oliver Twist?

20. What's special about the Lions House?

Now turn to the next page for the answers.

Answers to
Twenty Questions

1. King Edward I.
2. A bear.

3. Mute swans.
4. Over 24 years (24 years, 4 months and 4 days).
5. Lady Jerningham, on Meg's Mount.
6. Nine gun platforms.

7. Eggs.
8. Sallyport.
9. She saved nine people from a shipwreck.
10. Jimmy Strength.

11. Three of Berwick's eight bells.

12. In Holy Trinity church and churchyard.

13. He kept the keys of the gaol on Wallace Green.

14. No. It was built in 1816.

15. Two, Low Greens and High Greens.

16. The Scottish champion was killed.

17. A farrier fitted horseshoes.

18. A tripe dresser cleaned the stomach lining of an ox or cow before it was cooked and eaten.

19. Charles Dickens.

20. It has stone lions on the gateposts.

Other Places to Visit and Things to Do

A free map of Berwick and details of all these places are available from the Tourist Information Centre, 106 Marygate. Open all year.

In Berwick
Conundrum Farm Trail and Trout Fishing.

Swan Leisure Centre, Tweedmouth. Pool with flume and waves, other sports.

Summer *boat trips* on the River Tweed.

Summer *guided walks*, 'Time to Explore', start at the Tourist Information Centre.

In England (just)
Paxton House and Country Park with adventure playground.

On the Border
Union Chain Bridge at Horncliffe, crosses from England to Scotland.

In the Borough of Berwick upon Tweed
Chain Bridge Honey Farm near Horncliffe. Bees, hives and honey.

Heatherslaw Corn Mill. A working water mill on the River Till.

Heatherslaw Light Railway. Narrow gauge steam railway from Heatherslaw to Etal.

Etal Village, also 14th-century castle with audio tour – battles, banners and blood.

Ford Village. Lady Waterford Hall with murals; art gallery, pottery.

Milfield near Wooler. Full-scale copy of a Stone Age wooden henge or circle.

Lindisfarne (Holy Island) – cross by the causeway at low tide. Castle, Priory, Heritage Centre, birdwatching, walks.

Bamburgh. Castle, coast walks, Grace Darling Museum.

Seahouses. Boat trips to the Farne Islands.

Also

Alnwick. Some scenes from *Harry Potter and the Philosopher's Stone* were filmed at the castle, and there's a Water Garden with cascades and fountains. There's a huge second-hand bookshop in the old railway station.

The Tourist Information Centre at The Shambles is open all year.

Some other books published by **Luath** Press

Let's Explore Edinburgh Old Town
Anne Bruce English
Illustrations by Cinders McLeod
ISBN 0 946487 98 7 PB £4.99

 The Old Town of Edinburgh has everything. At the highest point is a huge castle. At the foot of the hill there's a palace.

Between them are secret gardens, a museum full of toys, a statue of the world-famous Greyfriars Bobby, and much more besides.

There were murders here too (think of Burke and Hare). There's mystery – is preacher John Knox really buried under parking space 44? And then there are the ghosts of Mary King's Close.

You can find out about all this and more in this guide. Read the tales of the Old Town, check out the short quizzes and the Twenty Questions page (all the answers are given), and you'll have plenty to see and do. Join Anne and Cinders on a fascinating and fun journey through time.

GENEALOGY
Scottish Roots: a step-by-step guide to tracing your Scottish ancestors
Alwyn James
1 84282 007 9 PB £9.99

HISTORY
A Word for Scotland
Jack Campbell
0 946487 48 0 PB £12.99

Old Scotland New Scotland
Jeff Fallow
0 946487 40 5 PB £6.99

Notes from the North
Incorporating a brief history of the Scots and the English
Emma Wood
0 946487 46 4 PB £8.99

Reportage Scotland
Louise Yeoman
0 946487 6 8 PB £9.99

A Passion for Scotland
David R. Ross
1 84282 019 2 PB £5.99

Plaids & Bandanas: Highland drover to Wild West cowboy
Rob Gibson
0 946487 88 X PB £7.99

LANGUAGE
Luath Scots Language Learner [Book & CD]
L Colin Wilson
0 946487 91 X PB £9.99
1 84282 026 5 CD £16.99

ON THE TRAIL OF
On the Trail of Robert Service
G Wallace Lockhart
0 946487 24 3 PB £7.99

On the Trail of William Wallace
David R Ross
0 946487 47 2 PB £7.99

On the Trail of Mary Queen of Scots
Keith Cheetham
0 946487 50 2 PB £7.99

On the Trail of Robert Burns
John Cairney
0 946487 51 0 PB £7.99

On the Trail of Robert the Bruce
David R Ross
0 946487 52 9 PB £7.99

On the Trail of John Muir
Cherry Good
0 946487 62 6 PB £7.99

On the Trail of Bonnie Prince Charlie
David R Ross
0 946487 68 5 PB £7.99

On the Trail of Queen Victoria in the Highlands
Ian R Mitchell
0 946487 79 0 PB £7.99

On the Trail of the Pilgrim Fathers
Keith Cheetham
0 946487 83 9 PB £7.99

On the Trail of John Wesley, founder of Methodist Church
J Keith Cheetham
1 84282 023 09 PB £7.99

THE QUEST FOR
The Quest For Arthur
Stuart McHardy
1 84282 012 5 HB £16.99

The Quest For The Celtic Key
Karen Ralls-MacLeod and Ian Robertson
0 946487 73 1 4 HB £18.99
1 84282 031 1 PB £8.99

The Quest for the Nine Maidens
Stuart McHardy
0 946487 66 9 HB £16.99

The Quest for the Original Horse Whisperers
Russell Lyon
1 84282 020 6 HB £16.99

NATURAL WORLD
The Hydro Boys: pioneers of renewable energy
Emma Wood
1 84282 016 8 HB £16.99

Wild Scotland: the essential guide to finding the best of natural Scotland
James McCarthy
0 946487 37 5 PB £7.50

Wild Lives: Otters – On the Swirl of the Tide
Bridget MacCaskill
0 946487 67 7 PB £9.99

Wild Lives: Foxes – The Blood is Wild
Bridget MacCaskill
0 946487 71 5 PB £9.99

Scotland – Land & People: An Inhabited Solitude
James McCarthy
0 946487 57 X PB £7.99

The Highland Geology Trail
John L Roberts
0 946487 36 7 PB £4.99

'Nothing but Heather!'
Gerry Cambridge
0 946487 49 9 PB £15.00

Red Sky at Night
John Barrington
0 946487 60 XPB £8.99

Listen to the Trees
Don MacCaskill
0 946487 65 0 PB £9.99

ISLANDS
Easdale, Belnahua Seil, & Luing & Seil: The Islands that Roofed the World
Mary Withall
0 946487 76 6 PB £4.99

Rum: Nature's Island
Magnus Magnusson
0 946487 32 4 PB £7.95

LUATH GUIDES TO SCOTLAND
The North West Highlands: Roads to the Isles
Tom Atkinson
0 946487 54 5 PB £4.95

Mull and Iona: Highways and Byways
Peter Macnab
0 946487 58 8 PB £4.95

The Northern Highlands: The Empty Lands
Tom Atkinson
0 946487 55 3 PB £4.95

The West Highlands: The Lonely Lands
Tom Atkinson
0 946487 56 1 PB £4.95

South West Scotland
Tom Atkinson
0 946487 04 9 PB £4.95

TRAVEL AND LEISURE
Die kleine Schottlandfibel [Scotland Guide in German]
Hans-Walter Arends
0 946487 89 8 PB £8.99

Edinburgh's Historic Mile
Duncan Priddle
0 946487 97 9 PB £2.99

Pilgrims in the Rough: St Andrews beyond the 19th hole
Michael Tobert
0 946487 74 X PB £7.99

FOOD AND DRINK
Edinburgh and Leith Pub Guide
Stuart McHardy
0 946487 80 4 PB £4.95

The Whisky Muse
Collected and introduced by Robin Laing
Illustrated by Bob Dewar
0 946487 95 2 PB £12.99

WALK WITH LUATH
Walks in the Cairngorms
Ernest Cross
0 946487 09 X PB £4.95

Short Walks in the Cairngorms
Ernest Cross
0 946487 23 5 PB £4.95

The Joy of Hillwalking
Ralph Storer
0 946487 28 6 PB £7.50

Scotland's Mountains before the Mountaineers
Ian Mitchell
0 946487 39 1 PB £9.99

Mountain Days and Bothy Nights
Dave Brown/Ian Mitchell
0 946487 15 4 PB £7.50

Skye 360: walking the coastline
Andrew Dempster
0 946487 85 5 PB £8.99

SPORT
Ski & Snowboard Scotland
Hilary Parke
0 946487 35 9 PB £6.99

Over the Top with the Tartan Army
Andy McArthur
0 946487 45 6 PB £7.99

BIOGRAPHY
The Last Lighthouse
Sharma Krauskopf
0 946487 96 0 PB £7.99

Tobermory Teuchter: a first hand account of life on Mull in the early years of the 20th century
Peter Macnab
0 946487 41 3 PB £7.99

Bare Feet and Tackety Boots: a boyhood on the island of Rum
Archie Cameron
0 946487 17 0 PB £7.95

Come Dungeons Dark [Guy Aldred]
John Taylor Caldwell
0 946487 19 7 PB £6.95

SOCIAL HISTORY
Pumpherston: the story of a shale oil village
Sybil Cavanagh
1 84282 011 7 HB £17.99
1 84282 015 X PB £7.99

Shale Voices
Alistair Findlay
0 946487 78 2 HB £17.99
0 946487 78 2 PB £10.99

FOLKLORE
Scotland: Myth, Legend & Folklore
Stuart McHardy
0 946487 69 3 PB £7.99

Luath Storyteller: Highland Myths & Legends
George W Macpherson
1 84282 003 6 PB £5.00

Tales of the North Coast
Alan Temperley
0 946487 18 9 PB £8.99

Tall Tales from an Island [Mull]
Peter Macnab
0 946487 07 3 PB £8.99

The Supernatural Highlands
Francis Thompson
0 946487 31 6 PB £8.99

MUSIC, DANCE AND WEDDINGS

Fiddles and Folk
G Wallace Lockhart
0 946487 38 3 PB £7.95

Highland Balls and Village Halls
G Wallace Lockhart
0 946487 12 X PB £6.95

The Scottish Wedding Book
G Wallace Lockhart
1 84282 010 9 PB £12.99

POETRY

Blind Harry's Wallace
William Hamilton of Gilbertfield
0 946487 43 X HB £15.00
0 946487 33 2 PB £8.99

Caledonian Cramboclink: verse, broadsheets and in conversation
William Neill
0 946487 53 7 PB £8.99

Men and Beasts: wild men & tame animals
Val Gillies & Rebecca Marr
0 946487 92 8 PB £15.00

Poems to be read aloud
collected and introduced by Stuart McHardy
0 946487 00 6 PB £5.00

Scots Poems to be read aloud
collectit an wi an innin by Stuart McHardy
0 946487 81 2 PB £5.00

The Luath Burns Companion
John Cairney
1 84282 000 1 PB £10.00

The Whisky Muse: Scotch Whisky in Poem and Song
collected and introduced by Robin Laing
illustrated by Bob Dewar
0 946487 95 2 PB £12.99

Kate o Shanter's Tale & other poems
Matthew Fitt
1 84282 028 1 PB £6.99

Immortal Memories [of Robert Burns]
John Cairney
1 84282 009 5 HB £20.00

Madame Fifi's Farewell & other poems
Gerry Cambridge
1 84282 005 2 PB £8.99

Bad Ass Raindrop
Kokumo Rocks
1 84282 018 4 PB £6.99

Picking Brambles
Des Dillon
1 84282 021 4 PB £6.99

Sex, Death & Football
Alistair Findlay
1 84282 022 2 PB £6.99

CARTOONS

Broomie Law
Cinders McLeod
0 946487 99 5 PB £4.00

FICTION

Milk Treading
Nick Smith
0 946487 75 8 PB £9.99

The Strange Case of RL Stevenson
Richard Woodhead
0 946487 86 3 HB £16.99

But n Ben A-Go-Go
Matthew Fitt
1 84282 014 1 PB £6.99
0 946487 82 0 HB £10.99

Grave Robbers
Robin Mitchell
0 946487 72 3 PB £7.99

The Bannockburn Years
William Scott
0 946487 34 0 PB £7.95

The Great Melnikov
Hugh Maclachlan
0 946487 42 1 PB £7.95

The Fundamentals of New Caledonia
David Nicol
0 946487 93 6 HB £16.99

The Road Dance
John MacKay
1 84282 024 9 PB £9.99

Luath Press Ltd

committed to publishing
well written books worth reading

LUATH PRESS takes its name from Robert Burns, whose little collie Luath (*Gael.*, swift or nimble) tripped up Jean Armour at a wedding and gave him the chance to speak to the woman who was to be his wife and the abiding love of his life. Burns called one of *The Twa Dogs* Luath after Cuchullin's hunting dog in *Ossian's Fingal*. Luath Press grew up in the heart of Burns country, and now resides a few steps up the road from Burns' first lodgings in Edinburgh's Royal Mile. Luath offers you distinctive writing with a hint of unexpected pleasures.

ILLUSTRATION: IAN KELLAS

Most UK bookshops either carry our books in stock or can order them for you. To order direct from us, please send a £sterling cheque, postal order, international money order or your credit card details (number, address of card holder and expiry date) to us at the address below. Please add post and packing as follows: UK – £1.00 per delivery address; overseas surface mail – £2.50 per delivery address; overseas airmail – £3.50 for the first book to each delivery address, plus £1.00 for each additional book by airmail to the same address. If your order is a gift, we will happily enclose your ‚card or message at no extra charge.

Luath Press Limited
543/2 Castlehill
The Royal Mile
Edinburgh
EH1 2ND
Scotland
Telephone: 0131 225 4326 (24 hours)
Fax: 0131 225 4324
Email: gavin.macdougall@luath.co.uk
Website: www.luath.co.uk